Friday Night Video

Written by Tommy Watkins

After school, Ian went to the video store.

A new movie and a video game were now available at the Video Store.

He even had a coupon for a pizza. It was setting up for a great night.

Ian picked up the DVD, video game disk, and pizza and went home.

He took a bite of the pizza and tasted the crust, which was hard as a rock.

The video game disk
was scratched and
didn't work.

The DVD was even unwatchable.

With the night ruined, Ian found an old book on his shelf.

For the rest of the night, he found fun in reading the tales of the Arabian Nights.

Ian went to bed full of creativity and imagination from reading the Arabian Nights.

The End.